Con

Walking times shown are approximate and depend on fitness, weight of rucksack, weather, conditions underfoot and height climbed.

Level of Difficulty **1** = Easy, **3** = Moderate, **6** = Hard
All walks are shown on O.S. Explorer map No.OL2 Yorkshire Dales Southern & Western Areas.
Every effort has been made to ascertain the accuracy of the walks described, the description of a route or track is not necessarily a right of way.

Some abbreviations have been used in the text to shorten it and make it more concise: -
PF = Public Footpath   RT = Right   LT = Left   FB = Footbridge
CP = Car Park   m = metres   km = kilometres   °M = magnetic

Walkers are strongly advised to wear the appropriate clothing and footwear for these walks.
• Boots/walking shoes.
• Waterproof Jacket.
• Over trousers.
• Small Rucksack for food, drinks and spare clothing.
• Hat & Gloves.
• Compass & map.

ISBN 978-1-903568-48-4

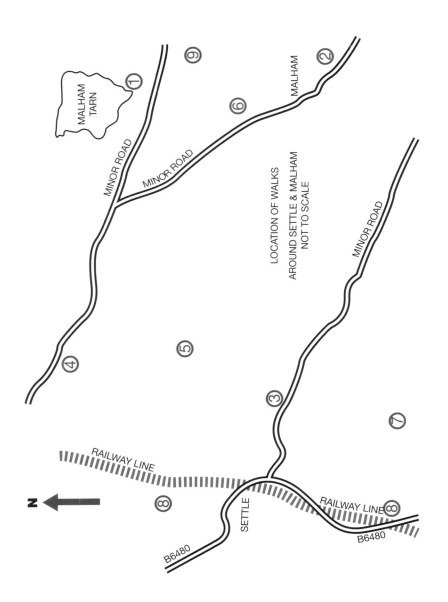

MALHAM TARN

①

⑨

②

MALHAM

⑥

MINOR ROAD

MINOR ROAD

LOCATION OF WALKS
AROUND SETTLE & MALHAM
NOT TO SCALE

MINOR ROAD

④

⑤

③

⑦

RAILWAY LINE

N

⑧

SETTLE

RAILWAY LINE

⑧

B6480

B6480

Walk 1 Malham Tarn Circular   **Distance** 6 miles/9.6 km
Start GR. 894658 Unmade CP 300m from Malham Tarn
Walk Time 2 hrs 45 min
Terrain A nice walk, with one steady ascent of 1.5km otherwise gently undulating with good views.

Leaving the unmade CP (**1**), head towards the tarn on the worn grass path. When you are near the tarn, turn RT and walk to the RT of a wood you see close by the tarn 300m ahead. Keep the stone wall just to your LT as you walk across grass to a farm gate.

Go through the gate and stay on the access track (it is also the Pennine Way), to the large house at the far side, which is Malham Tarn Field Studies Centre. Continue around the back of the building to descend the track on the far side (**2**).

You descend towards the tarn again on the access RD through the wood and pass all the old houses then cross a cattle grid. Ignore the sign for Pennine Way, and continue on the access track. As you pass the last house, there is a track on your LT and a post box in the wall there. Bear LT there along a narrow track.

Stay on this track for 500m until you reach the minor RD at the far end. Walk on the RD to where it forks and take the LT fork, signed Malham. Continue past High Trenhouse Centre (**3**) and when you reach the crossroads 300m further, cross to a PF sign pointing across a field to Langcliffe.

Continue across the field towards a wood ahead on the narrow worn grass path. You go through a gate in the stone wall as you slowly ascend keeping the broken stone wall on your RT side. You see a farm off to your RT by the RD. As you near the top of the hillside near Black Hill, you go through another gate in the wall (**4**).

Continue on the worn path now descending towards a track 600m ahead. On reaching the track, turn LT on it and walk for 2.8km until you emerge on a RD at Langscar Gate. Cross the cattle grid there (**5**) then bear off RT across the grass following the PF sign towards Waterlinks RD.

Walk over the hillside on the grass path between the limestone outcrops then the path bears RT through an opening in the stone wall. Cross the field, and go around the limestone outcrop on Dean Moor Hill. The path winds round back to the RD and the CP, which you should see ahead.

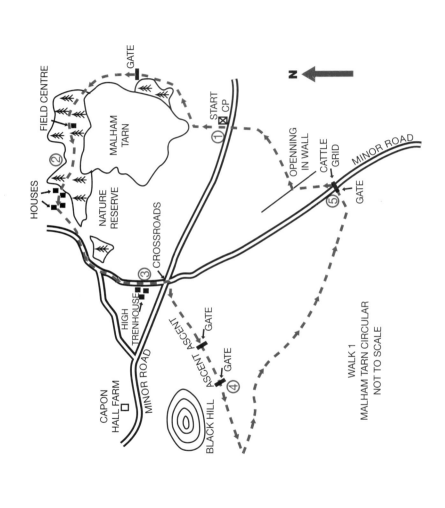

N

FIELD CENTRE

GATE

MALHAM TARN

START
CP
①

HOUSES

②

OPENNING
IN WALL

CATTLE
GRID

MINOR ROAD

GATE

⑤

NATURE
RESERVE

CROSSROADS

③

HIGH
TRENHOUSE

ASCENT ASCENT

GATE

GATE

④

CAPON
HALL FARM

MINOR ROAD

BLACK HILL

WALK 1
MALHAM TARN CIRCULAR
NOT TO SCALE

**Walk 2 Janet's Foss & Kissing Gates Walk Distance 3 miles/ 4.8 km
Start GR. 901628 The Buck Inn, Malham Village.
Walk Time 1 hr
Terrain A short steep ascent/descent on the minor RD then an
excellent, easy walk through a copse and between fields, back to
Malham. A good family walk!**

Leaving from The Buck Inn in Malham (**1**), cross the RD and go over
the small bridge and ascend the RD following the sign towards Malham
Tarn. Continue on the RD and pass The Lister Arms Hotel and Malham
YH. Leaving the village, follow the sign towards Gordale. The RD
ascends then descends the hillside.

Just before the bridge crossing Gordale beck, look for a ruined
building on a bend in the RD (**2**) at GR. 912634. Turn RT through a
kissing gate opposite, following the sign to Janet's Foss.

Continue on the path descending through the wood know as Janet's
Foss as you pass a nice waterfall. Following this path back to
Malham, you go through 9 kissing gates. Stay on the path by the
beck and you soon emerge out of the wood on a nice flat walk by the
beck and over fields (**3**). Your path winds round to Malham and you
go over a FB, which takes you back to your original starting point.

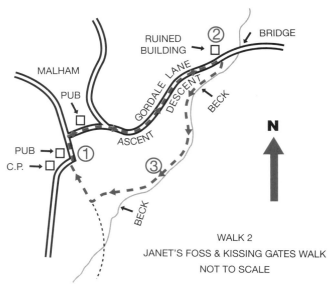

Walk 3 High Hill Circular   **Distance** 3.5 miles/5.7 km
Start GR. 820634 Greenfoot Town Centre Car Park, Settle.
Walk Time 1 hr 30 min

Terrain After a steep ascent on the RD, there is a very nice walk
on grass, over the hillside with fine views on route back to Settle.

Walk along passing North Ribblesdale RUFC (**1**) on Ingfield Lane
then at the junction by the Greenfoot CP sign on the corner, turn LT
and walk 120m to the top of the lane. Keep on the RD bearing LT
then at the top on Ingfield Lane, ascend to a small green area by a
telephone box (**2**). Turn RT there, walking steeply up the RD and as
you leave the village, you meet another RD on your LT.

Cut across to the RD at the far side and follow the sign for Kirkby
Malham, ascending the RD steeply for 1km. As you get to the top
of the RD, look for a PF sign on the LT and cross stone steps over
the wall (**3**) following the sign for Attermire Scar, GR. 832632.
The hill on the LT is High Hill, and you walk anticlockwise around
it on the cut grass path.

As you approach a minor RD (**4**), keep LT round High Hill. Ahead
is Sugarloaf Hill and you walk just to the LT of it then bear RT to
a gate in the fence at the far side. Limestone escarpments are all
around. Follow the cut grass path descending to steps over the wall
then bear LT ascending on grass keeping close by a stone wall.

After 400m, the path bears RT (**5**) towards the escarpments as you
walk keeping a wall just to your RT.

At the end of the wall descend the hillside ahead on the grass for
600m to join another track (**6**), turning LT, descend into Settle.

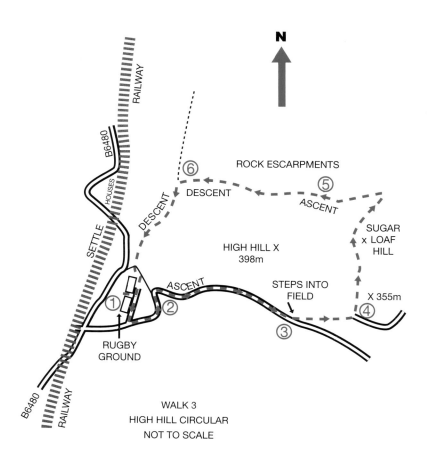

N

RAILWAY

B6480

RUGBY
GROUND

HOUSES

SETTLE

RAILWAY

B6480

RAILWAY

ROCK ESCARPMENTS

⑥ DESCENT

DESCENT

⑤

ASCENT

SUGAR
x LOAF
HILL

HIGH HILL X
398m

ASCENT

②

①

STEPS INTO
FIELD

③

X 355m

④

WALK 3
HIGH HILL CIRCULAR
NOT TO SCALE

Walk 4 Catrigg Force Waterfall Walk   **Distance 4.4 miles/7.1 km**
Start GR. 851678 On the minor RD near Westside House (farm).
Walk Time 2 hrs
Terrain Starting as a flat walk, you have a steep ascent from Cowside to the top of the hill then undulating to the finish. Some nice views from the hilltop and of the waterfall.

Cross to the PF sign opposite the access RD to Westside House (1) and go through the farm gate, walking diagonally and following the sign to 'Cowside ¾ mile'. You should soon see Cowside farm in the valley with trees surrounding it.

Cross diagonally over several fields (2) through gates and over stiles, still in the same direction towards Cowside.

You eventually go through a gate leading onto the minor RD. Turn RT on the RD and descend to the farm and ascend the RD behind it. On the top of the hill you come to a cattle grid (3). Continue over that on the RD, and 100m before you come to the next cattle grid, turn RT to go over another cattle grid (4) and down the winding RD towards Upper Winskill.

You should see the houses in the valley. On reaching Upper Winskill, a sign states Catrigg Force. Turn RT, following the sign and walking along by a wall keeping it on your LT (5).

Go through a farm gate keeping the wall still on your LT. The wall turns away as you follow a worn path across a field to a ladder stile. Cross then descend the track towards the wood at the bottom. Go through a farm gate then if you wish to visit the waterfall at Catrigg Force, follow the sign there, going through the second gate on your RT. Return to this spot after visiting the waterfall and take the middle gate just to your LT.

Walk along keeping the wall on your RT and cross a ladder stile in the corner of the field at GR. 834671. Turn LT to walk down to a FB (6). Cross, and follow the feint path ascending gently over the fields on a general bearing of 40°M from the FB towards the RD. Go through openings in the walls or over ladder stiles (7) at the far side of each field, heading towards your start point, which you should see ahead.

You see a barn ahead. Look for a ladder stile nearby as you head towards the concealed minor RD. Once you reach the RD, turn RT to walk back to your starting point 800m further.

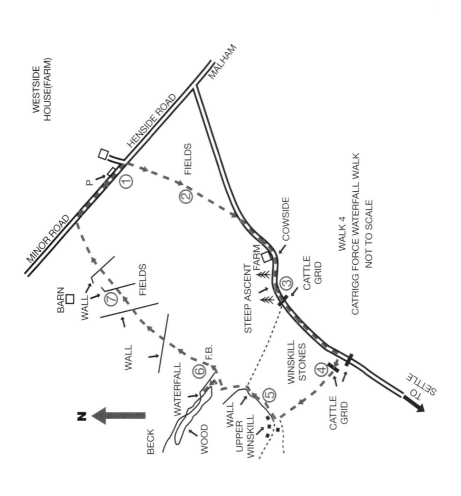

WESTSIDE
HOUSE (FARM)

HENSIDE ROAD

MALHAM

MINOR ROAD

P

① ②

FIELDS

COWSIDE

STEEP ASCENT

FARM

③ CATTLE
GRID

BARN

WALL ⑦

FIELDS

WALL

WALL

WATERFALL

⑥ F.B.

BECK

WOOD

WINSKILL
STONES

④ CATTLE
GRID

TO
SETTLE

⑤

UPPER
WINSKILL

WALL

N

WALK 4
CATRIGG FORCE WATERFALL WALK
NOT TO SCALE

Walk 5 Sugar Loaf Hill & Caves Walk   **Distance 5** miles/8 km
Start GR. 820634 Greenfoot Town Centre CP, Settle.
Walk Time 2 hrs
Terrain After a steep ascent on the RD, there is a very nice walk, mostly on grass, passing numerous caves, with good views over the area. A nice walk back into Settle.

Walk along passing North Ribblesdale RUFC on Ingfield Lane then at the junction by the Greenfoot CP sign on the corner (**1**), turn LT and walk 120m to the top of the lane. Keep LT again for 150m on Ingfield Lane, ascending to a small green area by a telephone box on the RT.. Turn RT there, walking steeply up the RD and as you leave the village, you meet another RD on your LT.

Cut across to the RD at the far side and follow the sign for Kirkby Malham, ascending the RD steeply for 1km. As you get to the top of the RD, look for a PF sign on the LT, GR. 832632 and cross stone steps over the wall (**2**) following the sign for Attermire Scar. The hill on the left is High Hill, and you walk anticlockwise around it on the cut grass path.

Walk around the hillside and as you approach a minor RD, keep LT round High Hill on the grass path.

Ahead is Sugar Loaf Hill (**3**) and you walk just to the LT of it and bear RT to a gate in the fence at the far side, GR. 838641. Limestone escarpments are all around. Follow the cut grass path descending to steps over the wall then bear RT then LT (**4**) between the escarpments, walking anticlockwise. Cross a ladder stile 150m ahead at GR. 839642 and continue along a hanging valley with the hillside rising steeply on your RT. There are many caves all around this area.

You come to a kissing gate, go through to walk with a wall just on your LT. Go through another kissing gate further along and walk now on a track for 200m to a ladder stile over a wall (**5**) on the LT, GR. 837655, where the track bends round. A number of caves are situated all around the area. Cross the ladder stile then follow the worn grass path descending to Clay Pits Plantation and a cattle grid.

Cross then walk 100m to the bend in the RD ahead (**6**). Turn LT on the RD, up through a gate by the wood following the sign to Settle. There are good views from the hills as you walk on the grass track past the wood. Continue cutting across the hillside towards another small wood on the lower slopes.

You come to the wood and continue in same direction towards Settle. Cross ladder stiles and through gates as you walk along the hillside towards Settle (**7**). Soon you walk with a wall on your RT, GR. 825647 as you approach Settle. There are good views of Settle from the hillside before the track descends into Settle centre. Walk through between the houses and back to Greenfoot CP where you started.

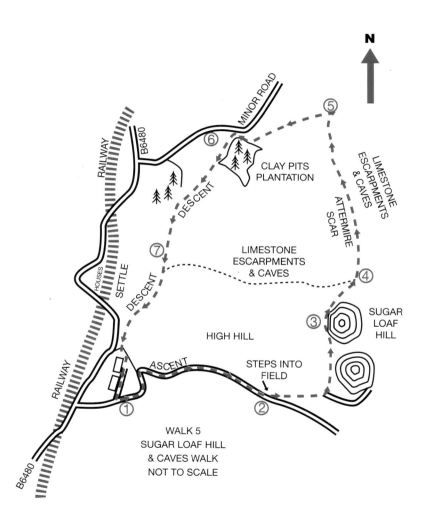

N

RAILWAY

B6480

MINOR ROAD

⑤

LIMESTONE ESCARPMENTS & CAVES

⑥

CLAY PITS PLANTATION

DESCENT

ATTERMIRE SCAR

HOUSES

SETTLE

⑦

LIMESTONE ESCARPMENTS & CAVES

④

DESCENT

③

SUGAR LOAF HILL

RAILWAY

HIGH HILL

ASCENT

STEPS INTO FIELD

①

②

B6480

WALK 5
SUGAR LOAF HILL
& CAVES WALK
NOT TO SCALE

Walk 6 Pikedaw Hill & Malham Cove Circular
Distance 5.3 miles/ 8.5 km
Start GR. 900627 CP 200m from Malham Village Centre
Walk Time 3 hrs
Terrain An easy start but becoming much harder as you ascend steeply up the hillside. From the top there is a gradual descent to the cove then a steep descent into Malham. Excellent views.

Leave the main CP in Malham (**1**), walk past The Buck Inn in the village centre and pass the telephone box on your RT. Continue to Beck Hall B&B where there is a bridleway on your LT between two stone walls. You soon come to a track where you turn LT then RT on the track.

Continue on the track keeping the wall on your RT and wire fence on your LT. Where you come to a fork in the track, take the LT fork and continue on the track passing several stone barns.

Before the sharp LH bend in the track, look for stone steps in the wall on your RT by a PF sign (**2**), taking you over the wall and diagonally across a field towards a barn at the far side at GR. 890633. Cross a stream and walk around to the far side of the barn as you start a 2km steep ascent to the top of the hill. You pass Hoober Edge and Hanber Side limestone escarpments as you ascend steeply.

Cross some steps in the wall and continue on the worn grass path to the top. Cross more steps in the wall and you see a small wooden post in the ground. Pass that and walk to 100m further to just past a flat limestone pavement. Look for the stone and grass wide track that runs from LT to RT at GR. 878640 (**3**).

Turn RT on this track and continue for 1.7km to emerge on a RD through a farm gate. Turn LT on the RD and walk for 1km to a cattle grid (**4**). Look for a PF sign pointing RT to Malham Cove. Descend the field by the wall and walk down into the gully onto the flat path at the bottom, which is The Pennine Way.

Continue on this path emerging at the top of Malham Cove and the limestone pavement there. After viewing the cove from the top, bear RT over the limestone pavement (**5**) and head towards the RD. Look for a worn path in the grass, leading to a gate on your LT on the top of the cove. Walk down a flight of stone steps descending the side of the cove to emerge at the foot of it by Malham Beck.

After viewing this area, continue on the tourist path by the beck, which leads back into Malham Village.

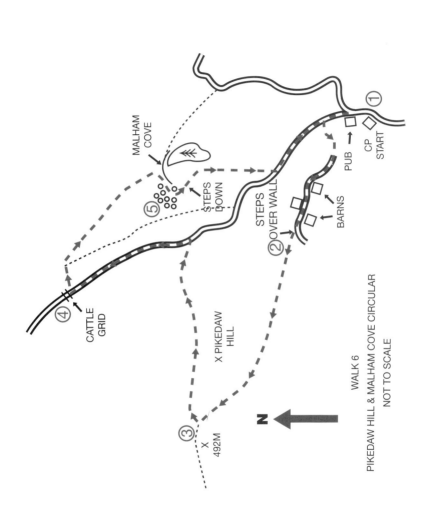

WALK 6
PIKEDAW HILL & MALHAM COVE CIRCULAR
NOT TO SCALE

N

① CP START
PUB
② OVER WALL
BARNS
STEPS
MALHAM COVE
STEPS DOWN
⑤
CATTLE GRID
④
X PIKEDAW HILL
③
X 492M

Walk 7 Cleatop Park Round   **Distance** 5.6miles/9.1 km
Start GR. 820634 Greenfoot Town Centre CP, Settle.
Walk Time 2 hrs 20 min
Terrain An excellent walk with good views especially from the higher ground. Some ascents/descents but not too demanding on grass and small stone tracks.

Walk along by North Ribblesdale RUFC on Ingfield Lane then at the junction by the Greenfoot CP sign (**1**), turn LT and walk 120m to a PF sign pointing RT along by a house. Walk along between the 2 stone walls and soon you go through a kissing gate. Continue on that track as you emerge by Hoyman Laithe Farm. Turn LT on the access track, ascending to Lodge Farm (**2**).

Go through the gate by the farm then bear LT on a winding track crossing a stream. You ascend sharply towards trees and over a ladder stile to pass Hudsa Plantation on your RT. Continue on the winding path then as you reach the large forest (Black's Plantation) ahead, follow the track turning RT.

You are now walking on a track passing the plantation off to your LT, then leading over the moor (**3**). Continue until you see a barn on the LT side of the track. Approx 80m before you reach the barn, cross a step stile (**4**) over a fence on your RT leading to Mearbeck.

Descend the track in the field with the stone wall on your LT towards a wood. As you descend, cross a ladder stile further down on your LT and cross a field still descending to the trees at the far RT. The path descends to a farm as you go through an opening in the wall and walk round to the RT of it and onto the access track.

Continue descending the access track until you are nearing the last houses near the bottom. Cross a step stile just before the tarmac part of the access track near the bottom and cross the field behind the house and through a gate into Mearbeck Wood. Walk through to the far side where the next large wood is ahead.

Cross the field to the RT corner and descend over the beck then follow the worn grass path to ascend straight along just below Cleatop Park wood (**5**), keeping the boundary wall to your RT. Near the end of the wood, continue with the by-pass below on your LT. Cross steps over the stone wall and follow the worn path through an opening then over several stiles as you cross fields back to Hoyman Laithe Farm (**6**). Emerging by the farm, walk on the track just to the RT of the farm on your original path taking you back into Settle and the CP.

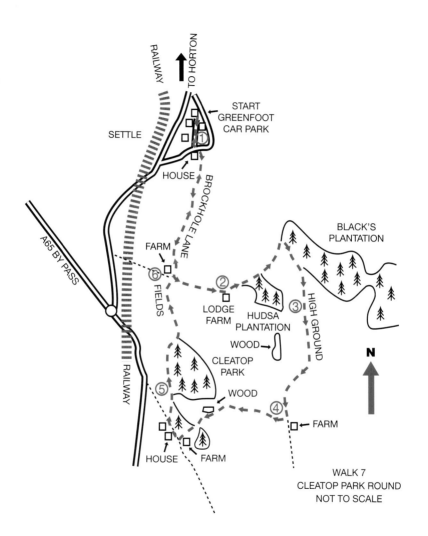

RAILWAY

TO HORTON

START
GREENFOOT
CAR PARK

SETTLE

①

HOUSE

BROCKHIOLE LANE

A65 BY PASS

FARM

⑥

FIELDS

②

LODGE
FARM

BLACK'S
PLANTATION

HUDSA
PLANTATION

③

HIGH GROUND

WOOD

RAILWAY

CLEATOP
PARK

⑤

WOOD

④

FARM

N

HOUSE

FARM

WALK 7
CLEATOP PARK ROUND
NOT TO SCALE

Walk 8 Settle Round   **Distance 6.2miles/10 km**

Start GR. 820634 Greenfoot Town Centre CP, Settle.

Walk Time 2 hrs 50 min

Terrain An excellent walk on grass and by the river, mostly flat apart from 2 short steep ascents. Good views from the hillsides.

Walk along by North Ribblesdale RUFC on Ingfield Lane then at the junction by the Greenfoot CP sign, turn LT and walk 120m to a PF sign pointing RT along by a house(**1**). Walk along between the 2 stone walls and soon you go through a kissing gate.

Continue on that track as you emerge by Hoyman Laithe Farm, then turn RT on the access lane which leads down to the B6480 RD. Cross the railway bridge (**2**) then the RD with care. Continue on the tarmac RD at the far side leading down past houses to the River Ribble. Turn LT then go through a kissing gate and over the bridge to the far side to descend again to the river.

You now have a good flat, but nice walk close by the river (**3**) for over 2 miles. Continue by the river, passing Brigholme Farm. You see a green bridge as you approach houses. Crossing a field, go through a small gate onto the RD then cross to the street opposite. Walk through the small housing development to an opening at the far end then along by the side of a house. This soon leads back to the riverside.

You are now walking alongside the sports fields. Continue by the river to a bridge by a school. Ascend to the RD, cross and walk again on the path at the far side as it leads away from the riverbank and across a field. Soon you emerge on a minor RD and turn RT to walk into the village of Stackhouse. You see a white painted house ahead. Walk just past it then turn RT along a track following a PF sign pointing to Locks (**4**). Cross a FB and ascend the lane to the main RD. Cross over the RD with care then cross the wooden FB over the railway line. Turn immediately LT at the far side and walk 100m along a track to go through 2 small gates. Ascend the hillside (**5**) for 200m keeping the wall just on your LT. You go through a gate at the top onto a track. Turn RT to walk into Langcliffe Village.

At a fork in the village, bear LT walking to the church then walk to the LT of it, going through a gate beside the Langcliffe sign on the RT. The path ascends RT, as you walk closely by the wall, looking down over Langcliffe (**6**). Cross ladder stiles and through gates as you walk along the hillside towards Settle. There are good views of Settle from the hillside before the track descends (**7**) into Settle centre. Walk through between the houses and back to Greenfoot CP where you started.

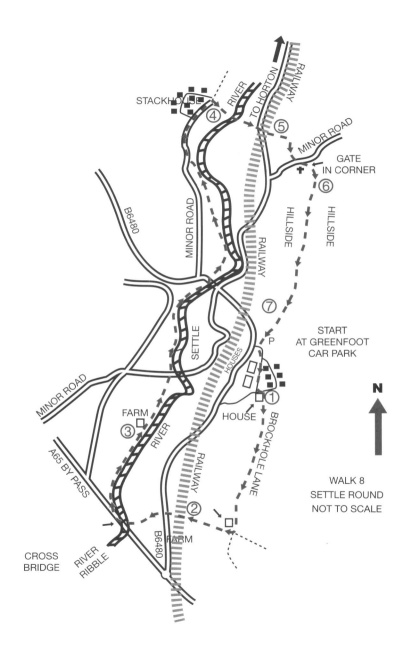

STACKHOUSE

RIVER

TO HORTON

RAILWAY

④

⑤

MINOR ROAD

GATE
IN CORNER

⑥

B6480

MINOR ROAD

HILLSIDE

HILLSIDE

RAILWAY

SETTLE

⑦

P

START
AT GREENFOOT
CAR PARK

HOUSES

MINOR ROAD

FARM

③

RIVER

HOUSE

①

BROCKHOLE LANE

N

A65 BY PASS

RAILWAY

②

WALK 8
SETTLE ROUND
NOT TO SCALE

CROSS
BRIDGE

RIVER
RIBBLE

B6480

FARM

Walk 9 Gordale Scar & Roman Camp Walk **Distance 7.95 miles/12.8 km**
Start GR. 901628 The Buck Inn, Malham Village.
Walk Time 3 hrs 45 min
Terrain A steep climb first up the minor RD then up Gordale Scar, not for the novice or in times of heavy rain, otherwise a very pleasant, gently undulating walk with good views.

Leaving from The Buck Inn in Malham (1), cross the RD and go over the small bridge and ascend the RD following the sign towards Malham Tarn. Continue on the RD and pass The Lister Arms Hotel and Malham YH.

Leaving the village, follow the sign towards Gordale. The RD ascends then descends the hillside before crossing Gordale Beck and the bridge there. Walk 110m past the bridge and before the farm, turn LT off the RD towards Gordale Scar (2), going through a gate. You are now walking on an obvious path towards Gordale Scar. When you reach the waterfall (3), scramble up the left of the main waterfall. Look for the hand and foot holes. The rocks can be wet and slippery at times. This part should not be attempted in times of flood or heavy rain, when you should use the alternative path shown on the sketch. Once up the first level, cross to the LT of the water and ascend the flight of steps to the top.

On the top of the Scar, walk on the grass with the stone wall just to your RT and the beck below it. Continue in the same direction for 1.5km until you come to a RD (4) on your LT. Cross onto the RD over the steps and turn RT, walking to an open, flat area and a LT hand bend in the RD at GR. 904657.

At this bend, turn RT, going through a farm gate then walk diagonally LT across the field (5) on a feint path, bearing 38°M from the gate. You may see Malham Tarn well off to your LT. Ascend then descend the hillside to the lower part at the far side of the field.

Go through a gate at GR. 910664 and keep the stone wall closely on your RT as you cross the beck then ascend to a ladder stile after 220m. Cross the stile (6) and follow the feint path over the grass hillside called High Stony Bank. After 1km, the path winds towards a wall as you pass the site of a former Roman camp.

As you come to the track by the wall, continue on it until you come to a farm gate and wall ahead. Go through the gate then immediately RT through another gate (7).

Descend the undulating field keeping a wall to your RT. Keep in the same direction until you go through a farm gate by Middle Laithe Farm, emerging on a minor RD. Turn RT (8) on the undulating RD and stay on it for 3.5km, descending into Malham.

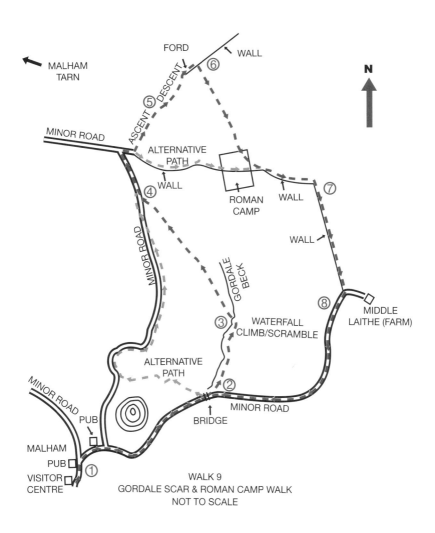

MALHAM TARN

N

FORD

WALL

⑥

DESCENT

ASCENT

⑤

MINOR ROAD

ALTERNATIVE PATH

WALL

④

ROMAN CAMP

WALL

⑦

WALL

MINOR ROAD

GORDALE BECK

WALL

③

WATERFALL CLIMB/SCRAMBLE

⑧

MIDDLE LAITHE (FARM)

ALTERNATIVE PATH

②

MINOR ROAD

MINOR ROAD

PUB

BRIDGE

MALHAM

PUB

①

VISITOR CENTRE

WALK 9
GORDALE SCAR & ROMAN CAMP WALK
NOT TO SCALE

Notes